Text
Murray Ball

Production
John Barnett
Pat Cox

Production Assistants
Maria Kenny
Tim Carthew

Cel Photography
Bob Evans

Book Design
Brian Moss

Design Assistant
Marcel Tromp

© Visual material copyright On the Ball Productions Ltd & Co 1986
© Text copyright Diogenes Designs Ltd 1986

All Rights Reserved. No part of this publication may be reproduced, stored in a retrieval system or transmitted in any form or by any means, electronic, mechanical, photocopying, recording or otherwise without the prior permission of the Copyright Owners.

ISBN 0-86464-077-3

Created and Produced by Magpie Productions Ltd.
Printed and published by Inprint Limited,
Eastern Hutt Road,
Lower Hutt,
New Zealand
for
Magpie Productions Ltd.

THIS IS ME. i.e. The Grey Ghost of the Forest, The Scarlet Manuka, The Iron Paw, The modest yet interesting Dog. The following are pictures of my adventure in which I beat the Mad Murphys, The Killer Croco Pigs, The Villainous Vernon The Vermin and draw with the Mighty and Magnificent Cat, Horse, which is pretty good eh?
p.s. Wal is also in it, and Cooch. Also one or two others too ~~insignifikant~~ ~~insigniph~~ yukky to mention. So into it!

Actually what I have learned is that Stars do not have much to say in what happens in a picture. The Producers do. So I will mention one or two other co-stars or the sods will cut me off without a scent. And what good is a noseless dog eh?
So here they are:-

COOCH
Cooch Windgrass. The only man I know who would make a decent sort of dog. Need I say more. To use Rangi's ~~eloqoant elekant~~ neat way of sayin' things — He's choice man. A strange boy, Rangi.

PONGO
Pongo. Wal's niece. Spoilt, private school, bossy. Throws tripe out of the window when no-one is looking which is her only good point.

RANGI
Rangi is a strange boy. For a long time he wanted to make me into a dog skin cloak. Wal talked him out of it by giving him one of his old footy jerseys which he reckons was more colourful and smelt better. I think I am insulted. Rangi lives up the road. He is quite good at footy.

WALLACE CADWALLADER FOOTROT
A gent. A man of infinite charm and wit. Happy, good natured and a born optomist. Never grizzles, never swears, never blames others for his own mistakes. A typical farmer. My very best mate and blood brother. The only bloke who can reach the dog tucker.

JESS
Cooch's bitch. We are just very, very good friends.

It is shearing time. This is Wal. Note the elegant pose. Poetry in motion.

Rangi Jones is fleeco. He believes that Wal's sheep would have been better shorn if it had backed into an aeroplane propeller. A stern critic.

Cooch showing his class. Animals love the bloke. We know quality when we see it.

There is not much good you can say about Aunt Dolly except that she makes beauty pikelets. Smoko time.

However the Grey Ghost of the Forest does not feast on soppy pikelets. Oh no Mate! It's nature in the raw for Grey Ghosts. Personally I like the way crutchings stick to your teeth. Doesn't do much for your breath though. Wal is inclined to be a little intolerant when it comes to table manners.

Pongo, useless as ever, calls for my help.

Unfortunately I was a little caught up.

However you cannot keep a good dog up. And The Dog is nothing if not gallant. I bound to her aid.

Curses, one moved!
While I am temporarily out of action trouble strikes. It's the Murphy boys in their helicopter.

Cooch and Wal tell Hunk and Spit what they can do with their Chopper.

But the villains have done their work. They stampede the sheep who burst the door and carry the heroic, yet slightly undignified Dog into the sheep dip.

The Dog in a spot of trouble.
In fact drowning.
My cool adventurous life flashes before my eyes.

This is me as a puppy. A rather cute little chap I always think.
Aunt Dolly is delivering me from her hell-hole of a Cats' Home
in Tauranga to Wal.

Wal at home. Footrot Flats. Morning. He runs a 'comfy' home.

Wal spots Aunt Dolly. The usual joy and jubilation. Decides to tidy up a little.

The cat, Horse, is not the easiest thing to tidy up.

But Wal still manages to present himself suave and well groomed on her arrival.

I meet Wal. A poignant moment. Then that foul-mouthed old chook decides to tell him my name.

A dog of metal can only do one thing. I try and strangle her. Unfortunately she is too GROSS but at least I slowed her down a bit.

Then that man of giant intellect and understanding does a wonderful thing. Ignoring his unspeakable ancestor, he looks me in the eye — man to man and calls me "Dog".
What a ripper eh?

I meet Major the Pig dog. (What no curly tail?) Ha Ha! Just kidding Major. He is big and tough and a hero — blast him.

I move into my 'kennel'. No T.V.

Little blokes like sucking things when they've had a hard day. First night in a spooky place is not the time to meet your first sheep skull.

I decide to take a stroll in the cool of the evening to think things over.

While lost in philosophical thought, I perceive someone bung a sack over the bridge.

I am not one to let pass the opportunity to do some good. I plunge resolutely into the raging torrent to retrieve the sack.

Further down stream Coochie is living it up as only he knows how — playing with eels. Coochie often appears mildly eccentric.

I swim powerfully over to Cooch with the bag.

Inside the bag is a puppy. It is quite neat. It has sort of dreamy eyes and a sort of wiggly walk which is also neat. Weird.

Cooch calls it JESS. Which I think is a neat name.

It is sort of friendly and warm. It gets a bit close which is weird. But quite neat actually.

Wal is a deeply sensitive man. He misses me. He thinks I am lost. What a nice bloke he is underneath.

I tell him I'm okay.

Wal is delighted but a bit embarrassed that he had shown Cooch he wasn't the hard case he always seemed to be.

About now I come out of my drowning dream. Dear old Wal is giving me the kiss of life. Noble fellow. However he reckons Major pulled me out of the dip. I tell him yeh, well I was only checking the sheeps' feet. Smart Alec, Major.

Cooch, Jess and I shoot off to Cooch's place where the Murphys' helicopter is after Cooch's deer.

That ratbag Spit Murphy is tryin' to net Cooch's stag. But Pew bombs him with a whitey and Coochie musters the herd into the house until the Murphy sods go away.

A dog of character does not allow deer rustling drongos to play the giddy goat on his patch. Jess and I follow the helicopter. I intend telling them a thing or two!

However the Murphys' place is a sort of green hell. Slime, crocopigs and blood. I decide to tell them a thing or two some other time . . . maybe.

Then a funny thing happened. Jess sort of changed. I discovered she was not a bloke but a blokess. I always knew that she was neat but suddenly she seemed even neater. Cripes!

On the way home that well known rugby genius, W. Footrot stopped off to give Rangi and Pongo a few pointers about the game. Rangi is not bad but too unorthodox Wal reckons.

However Rangi and Pongo tell Wal that an All Black selector will be watching his next game.

Wal likes the sound of that. He has always felt that his not being in the All Black team was some sort of terrible mistake. He dreams of demonstrating his prowess in a Test Match.

That blonde seductress Cheeky Hobson is there curse her. She would not be in *my* dream!

Wal goes into training. The only similarity between him and Rocky is he can drink raw eggs too. However he vomits better.

If Wal has one fault it is that he is a fool. After all the training he has done he is going to blow it on a night of debauchery with that fat chested Jezebel Cheeky Hobson.

The fool Wal being sucked in by Cheeky Hobson's Harem Nights body spray.

I plead. In vain. He is under the scented seductress's spell. Curse her!

Wal and Cheeky Hobson at their orgy at Pawai's Pie Cart.

I brood. I fear the worst. Who can blame me? I am quite sure she is bent on destroying his chances in the Big Game tomorrow. I suspect poison!

I decide to act. Is it not my duty? I leap upon the table and check his teacup for the poison pills I knew she dropped in.

How embarrassing. I can't find them! There is only one thing for a gentleman to do. I faint.

Cheeky is a bit upset. Snob. Vows she will never see Wal again. Stomps off. Pawai tries to smooth things over by offering pudding but Wal has the snots too and we push off.

He ties me under the walnut tree to guard the walnuts from the rats. He *knows* I hate that. Mean sod. Not a word of thanks.

The rats come. I warn them. Be off with you I say. But you cannot reason with some rats.

I defend valiantly. I bite here, I snap there. But it is difficult because I'm scared I might get one of those horrible tails in my mouth. YUK!

Then. Like a piebald avenging angel — the Cat called Horse.

He rips into them to such effect that the mangled remains take off back to the Murphys' place from whence they came. I'd done it. Well Horse and I had done it. Well. I was *there* while Horse did it . . .

The storm hit like a bursting bladder.

Meanwhile the Murphys hold an intellectual discussion on how to steal Coochie's stag.

The subtle plan is carried out and under cover of darkness and the storm, they seize and carry off Cooch's stag.

The storm builds into a fury. Water pours off the ranges. Slips slither down hills and the river becomes a brown bulldozer roaring across the land. Jess in her bitch's box is swept away.

Cooch feeding out hay to his deer herd notices the stag is missing.

Rangi, Wal and I are out moving the stock to higher ground. Rangi spots Jess's box smashed on the Murphys' side of the main river channel.

Now I'm not one to be critical of Wal as you know, but I reckon he should have listened to Rangi when he tried to tell him about Jess's box. But NO. Wal was off to become an All Black. Nothing else mattered.

But Jess is not drowned. She is cold and miserable in the storm. She slinks into the Murphys' outbuildings where it is comparatively warm and dry.

But would the Mighty Iron Paw leave her to her fate? No. Rang' and I decide to cross the raging river by the old swing bridge. The Iron Paw does not flinch from danger — The Iron Paw presses on regardless. The bloody silly Iron Paw is left all by himself on the Murphys' side of the river!

Rangi shoots off and tries to get Wal to rip over to the Murphys and rescue us. Well . . . Jess. Well . . . Jess and me, I suppose.

The Iron Paw does not let his tail droop for long. I push off to find Jess. Seeing her tracks leading up to the Murphys' place slows me down a bit. But the Iron Paw is as silly as the next dog and I press on.

I get a nasty shock. The Murphy hell hounds. I get a pleasant surprise. They are locked in their cage.

The Grey Ghost of the Forest has a sense of humour.

So does Fate.

Very funny Fate!

Fortunately I am fleet of foot and nimble of body, — and, to be honest, a bit lucky.

Behold the flight of the Grey Ghost.

While I am outwitting the Murphys' dogs, the All Black selector is running his eyes over the local football talent i.e. W. Footrot (The Fathead — why isn't he here?)

Wallace, ever one to seize an opportunity, demonstrates the form for which he has become justly famous . . .

But Fate once more steps in to stir up the works. The Raupo team fullback is scraped off the deck and carried off. Wal asks Rangi to play substitute. Rangi, sly kid, reckons if he can steal the ball he can get Wal to follow him to the Murphys' place.

Rangi havin' more footy talent in his little finger than the rest of the mugs on the paddock have in their whole bodies, scores the winning try for Raupo. He then takes off with the ball for the Murphys' farm.

It doesn't take him long to work out that he is not going to outrun the Murphys' Landrover. He manages to hop aboard from an overhanging bank. Irish Murphy spots him.

Remember Jess? She is in the cactus without boots. The stag shed she is sheltering in is the lair of the King Rat, known to his buddies as Vernon the Vermin. He's bad news.

Willing as I am to die for her, I have problems of my own. The Murphys' dogs have found me.

While I am preparing to mount a rescue (providing I am not eaten by the hellhounds), the cat Horse has put in an appearance at the stag shed. Horse versus a thousand rats. Good odds. Anyone's game.

The Murphys arrive. No doubt a little perplexed at the bedlam in their outbuildings.

I have with cool resourcefulness, or as Wal would call it, luck, landed on a log that as skill would have it hurtles down a shute, smashes through a couple of walls and pops Vernon the Vermin like a blood-filled tick between my log and a solid object — namely Hunk Murphy's head.

I rescue Jess and we beat a strategic retreat to the river. The mad Murphy shoots at us. The bullet breaks the wire holding the raft and sets us adrift.

Sore loser Irish Murphy has another go and hits Horse. He falls onto our raft. I am quite flattered. I've never had Horse drop in on me before.

The Murphys' crocopigs live along the river. They are dangerous and tough and eat dogs. Also all rubbish too horrible to go in even the Murphys' rubbish bins.

Am I afraid? Yes. But the Iron Paw does not let pigs eat neat young bitches without showing them where they get off. I give them the hiding they deserve.

But even I cannot outweigh half a tonne of uncooked bacon. Alas. Sometimes being a hero is not enough.

Fear not gentle reader. The Dog in the water is a fearsome enemy. I foil the powerful but dumb porkers and return, injured but brave to the raft. Jess licks the old wound. Cute kid.

Wal, intelligent as he is, remembers the river runs under the bridge. He and the kids leap to the rescue.

Pongo spots us. Rangi, brave lad, allows Wal to hang him over the side to hook us up. He grabs Jess.

But misses Horse and Me. The writhing, swirling ocean sucks us down its throat.

The Dog and Horse are dead. (Actually I was quite flattered to die with Horse). Two heroes gone.

Pongo and Rangi, although hard cases, also love The Dog Naturally. They do not want to leave the beach. Tears and gnashing of teeth.

Fooled you eh? Guess who?

There are a lot of things you can say Dog hasn't got — but class isn't one of them. What a climax.

They are delighted to see me.

The Dog is a hero. He beats Major and is almost as good as Horse.
(Actually Jess thinks I'm better — she is very nice and has extremely good taste).